D1527295

Effective SOPs

Make your standard procedures help your business become more productive

Disclaimer:

The author of this book has tried to present the most accurate information to his knowledge at the time of writing. This book is intended for information purposes only. The author does not imply any results to those using this book, nor are they responsible for any results brought about by the usage of the information contained herein.

No part of this book may be reprinted, electronically transmitted or reproduced in any format without the express written permission of the author.

Note – this book was previously published as 'Visual SOPs'.

Table of Contents

Do Your SOPs Help Your Business?

Welcome.

If you are reading this then I guess that you are as frustrated with Standard Operating Procedures (SOPs) as I have been in the past. Whilst SOPs can make a huge difference to a business they can also be a relic of a past time or a symbol of a Quality Management System created to give an image of order. If any of this rings a bell with you then, by the end of this short book, you should be in a far better position with a more usable and more effective approach to using this simple but powerful tool. SOPs are designed to help us remember. Instead we forget to complete all of the pre-determined eight steps and we end up wondering why the quality of our work isn't as great as it could be. This is even more evident within the office environment where we find that there are even more combinations and permutations compared to a manufacturing environment. We need to come up with a better way to create and use our SOPs. A simple solution is presented in this book.

We don't deliver on our promises as easily when we don't optimise the way we work. SOPs are there to take the best ideas we have in our business and create a simple document that allows everyone in the business to take advantage of this 'best practise'. When we get the right people writing the best method of working we can create a fabulous suite of tools that can make our lives easier.

When we choose not to create new SOPs on the back of our Continuous Improvement endeavours, life is made harder than it needs to be. We make life hard for ourselves by not capturing the new insights and information that we gather and then not integrating this into our working lives. This book discusses this and shares ideas on what to do next.

When we write SOPs that are too rigid we often find ourselves fighting against their inflexibility and end up avoiding using them. SOPs should provide accurate guidance and instructions and be practical and easy to follow with an appropriate level of rigidity. This will be discussed in this book too.

Some formats work better than others and it is up to us to find what works best. If you are familiar with the PDCA (Plan Do Check Act) or Continuous Improvement Cycle then you will be used to the idea of trialling ideas, working out what works and what doesn't, and iterating your ideas until you have found a format the serves you best. This short book includes links to five documents for you to download and use:

- A Microsoft PowerPoint based SOP format.
- A Microsoft Word based SOP format.
- A Microsoft Word sign off template.
- A Microsoft Excel example SOP register.
- A Microsoft PowerPoint 'SOP map'

The downloads aren't definitive, they are for you to use and alter as you see fit. If you dislike your current format, or if you haven't got a format you want to use they should help you on your journey.

So, SOPs are useful and should be highly beneficial to your business. By the end of this short book you should be better able to take advantage of what you do have and be able to implement a way of using SOPs that serves your business more effectively.

The Importance of SOPs

Quality is one of the main reasons that SOPs are introduced in the first place. You need to know the correct sequences of doing a particular task and the SOP becomes the place where this information is stored. Producing items, or delivering services, to the right level of quality is absolutely essential and is a basic requirement of being in business. The value of SOPs, however, is more than just this. This section of the book will look at a few different reasons that back up the view that you need to have workable SOPs present in your business.

One of the most striking reasons to use SOPs is to ensure that the knowledge we have in our business stays in our business. I'm not talking about industrial espionage, I am talking about the fact that the people who are doing the work today might not be here in a year's time (or a month for that matter). What is commonly referred to a 'tacit' knowledge needs to be routinely purged from the minds of our staff and recorded for the use of the business (also known as 'explicit' information). I'm sure that you have witnessed someone retire, for example, and watched as they took thirty plus years of information with them on the way out. Getting the right degree of information to be retained by the business is the key here, not to get bogged down with an administrative system that we become slaves to. We need to keep the right information working for our business, rather than forcing ourselves to go through a learning curve every time we get a new member of the team join us.

Processes can drift over time. When we get trained to undertake a process (whether this is working on a production line, chairing a Board meeting, or any other type of process in between) we often follow the discreet steps as prescribed until we gain confidence and knowledge about the process. Then as we continue to execute the process we can find ourselves trimming little bits here and there to accommodate our style. Having a flexible approach to SOP writing can allow for this, but the trouble comes when you have a time pressure in your way and you cut a corner 'just this once'. If there is no immediate repercussion then there is a risk that a new habit could be formed, what could be perceived as a streamlined version. The refreshing of SOPs gives us an opportunity to evaluate these changes in the context of the original specification and accept or reject the changes. Not reviewing the SOPs can allow these habits to exist and, if they don't serve the business correctly, they can cause longer term problems. I have seen this particular issue time and time again, and if the bad methods are allowed to propagate then operational performance issues can ensue.

Training new staff members up is one of the best internal reasons I can think of for having SOPs. Not having any guidelines for new members of staff just isn't fair. Have you seen new members of staff trying to make notes on their pads of paper whilst someone who is experienced (in their own way of doing the task and not the SOP route possibly) rattles through the entire sequence of actions? Although this might still be a preferred method of learning for many, backing it up with up to date SOPs can make the whole process a lot easier for everyone involved. When the information contained in the documents makes sense then the process of training can be made easier. It can take a lot of time up for the individuals who are training the new people, who then cut corners because they need to get on with their own work. Result? New people who don't quite understand the full extent of their jobs, trained in methods that don't quite follow the original procedures. We can do better than this and speed up the process of new members of staff becoming productive team members.

When we are trying to improve our businesses and want a 'fast flexible flow' through our business rework is one of the last things you want in your way. When looked at from a higher level (which we will later) SOPs should map out across an entire process from start to finish. When written and followed correctly the SOPs should prevent rework from having to take place. This effect is even more pronounced in the office environment. Administrative work often has more 'grey' involved if the work is not formalised and this can lead to later sections of the work (possibly undertaken by a different team within the business) to have to be completed or adjusted so that the next section can do their work. Combine this rework with a delay from the time which the work was originally done and you start to get a recipe for long delays. SOPs help to define the standards at each step in a process, whether you have multiple SOPs per process or one all-encompassing one, resulting in less rework / delays if followed correctly. Killing off delays is a central theme to the Lean improvement approach and one that SOPs can help with.

Some customers have specific requirements that are recorded within our SOPs. If you fail to enact these instructions then there could be consequences going forwards for your business. If we look over the last few paragraphs then we can see how this links in to the previous sections. Poor training that fails to teach people on specific requirements can be a recipe for disaster. Getting our SOPs into a state that is reflective of real practise, are easy to work with, and integrated into our working lives can help with adhering to our customer requirements. Like any other process within our businesses, if we can get our ways of working built into some kind of system that churns out the right kind of information at the right time, we have a better chance of improving our overall business performance than if we don't.

Following on from the PDCA reference in the introduction, the A for Act is a vital link between the work we do and the innovations we make with our SOPs. SOPs are brilliant for crystallising knowledge and help us to keep a degree of control over what we do with our workplace discoveries and their associated improvements. Granted there are other ways to 'Act' once we have made an improvement, but changing the standard instructions we provide to our workforce is certainly one of the main ones to consider. Of course there is an assumption here. The assumption is that many businesses follow something as simple and rigorous as the PDCA cycle (or DMAIC if you're more Six Sigma orientated). Many businesses do not have any kind of improvement strategy, let alone follow through on their improvements in any kind of substantial way. If you are looking for a good way to get your business improvement projects to have a chance at sticking longer term then inclusion of SOPs as part of the improvement's close out is worthy of significant consideration.

Finally, for this section, and leading on from the last point, SOPs need not only be the end point for improvements but for newly introduced processes. The amount of times I have seen new software tools implemented into a business, or seen a piece of machinery switched on, without supplementary instructions are staggering. Basic questions are often overlooked. From the software point of view 'how best do you navigate and use this software to ensure that your business gets the most out of it for your needs?' For machinery, 'how do you undertake the operator maintenance, so that your business gets the most out of the kit?' are questions that are well worth asking.

SOPs are important, I think you can agree, and their application is often wider than we appreciate. I hope that this section has given you some items to reflect upon and, if you have not included certain uses of SOPs in your current way of working, then has perhaps given you some ideas going forwards.

Why Do We Struggle with SOPs?

There are many reasons why we may struggle with SOPs. If your experience is anything like mine then you will realise that referring to SOPs is one of those things that tends to make people roll their eyes!

In fact, the first time I saw an SOP was in my first post in industry. A factory inspector had been onsite to see a couple of issues that the business was trying to address. One of those issues was in the department I was running, and I was completely in the dark as to their being an issue, the existence of the instructions (SOP), let alone the need for protective equipment. In retrospect I was the perfect 'patsy' to take this fall and with only having a week and a half's experience of running my department the factory inspector gave me a month to sort things out.

I dug out the SOP and it was awful, it was also crammed in the back of a dusty lever arch folder on a shelf in the back of a spraying area. The PPE was there too, covered in dust... Please rest assured that I did sort out the issue in my department, but it also gave me a wider understanding of how reliant businesses can be on the memories of their staff and how formal instructions within a business can easily get lost.

This section of the book is going to look at a few different reasons, in my opinion, as to why SOPs are not used effectively in the workplace.

Starting in the most obvious place, we have the issue that SOPs are usually not written by the best person. Instead of the person who does the job explaining some of the nuances and intricacies of doing the job, we end up with someone disconnected from the process writing the instructions. We end up with a battle between theory and practise. Theory usually loses and the job gets done anyway. I saw one business who, after realising that their SOPs weren't working wrote entirely new SOPs in a new format. And yes, there were several iterations of the SOPs. There was some good stuff in there, but the writing and the using of the SOPs were two completely distinct activities. Writing from the perspective of an Engineer I can attest to the fact that what you see from a design or management point of view can be significantly different from the position of an 'operator'. Getting the right people to provide an input to the writing of the documents is a specific point we'll come back to. The question I would ask you now is, 'who is writing your

SOPs?'

The next point is that SOPs, once written, are often forgotten about. Their use in the business is not linked directly to other things that we do and so it becomes easy to not use them (or hard to keep using them, depending on your point of view). Creating a formal way of attaching your SOPs to your day to day working is something that we will specifically look at later. Integrating these instructional documents into our normal working life not only makes SOPs easier to access and refer to, but actually makes the idea of these tools become normal. We need to make SOPs central to the way we work as opposed to the appendage that they are frequently made to be.

So, the next question is 'how discrete are your SOPs, are they part of your day to day?'

Finally, another point to consider is the notion of SOPs not being managed as a process in their own right. Again, this is all about standard operating procedures becoming part of the normal way of working. A common observation is for a business to operate with out of date instructions. Not only do these documents have details of practises that are no longer followed, but even worse they include a revision date that has clearly passed. By combining a simple 'process management' approach to SOPs and connecting this to a business habit you can make the management and updating of SOPs a relatively straightforward activity. Finding the right person in your organisation to manage the revision control and updating process is often a challenge. Most businesses that I have experienced have a central staff member, such as a Quality Engineer, responsible for the SOP register. I recall many times as a Manufacturing Engineer where I would annually review specific examples from our Quality Engineer's auditing list. I was always one step behind the audit because of the scale of the task and the Quality Engineer's ability to choose obscure SOPs that hadn't been reviewed in the past year (probably 15 years is more accurate). Although I maintained the master SOPs in a neat filing system behind my desk it was not my sole responsibility to maintain the information contained within the masters. In fact, it was not part of the business' conscious and so no one did it. Putting this focus into a senior manager's job description, to cascade the importance into the day to day routine of working can help to get the right approach. Ultimately you will decide what the right approach will be for your business, and again, we will look into this subject and explore some ideas later in this book.

So, the final question in this section 'who is responsible for keeping the importance of SOPs alive in your business?'

Visual versus Text Only

There are many SOPs written as purely text documents, I'm sure that you have seen these on your travels. This section is going to look at using more visual SOPs in your business. Whether you already use visual based SOPs or not, I hope that you get some ideas on what kind of format would suit the products and services that you need to deliver in your quest for effective SOP documentation.

The best point I can make about using visuals in a document of this nature goes back to my time as a Production Engineer. We had just finished the installation of a new process line, based on a sister factory's technology, and the instructions needed to be written for the operation of the equipment. There were a lot of valves and pipes and gauges to include in the step by step instructions and on one Friday morning I wrote down all of the steps required to operate the equipment. We had someone working with us who was from our sister factory and so they thankfully helped us list out the correct sequence. By the end of the morning we had completed our task, I wrote up the steps on the computer and our foreign colleague set off on his journey home.

Monday morning came round and I ventured into the production area where we were about to start up the machinery. The only problem was that when we read our own instructions and attempted to get the machine to start we couldn't figure out what we needed to do in what order!

There were lots of valves, valves that were unlabelled on our machinery, referred to in our instructions. We were stumped by our own instructions.

As we knew what the machine was meant to do and how it was meant to do it we could figure it out from an engineering perspective, which was no use to the operators who stood there and smiled to themselves as a colleague and I worked out the sequence of operation once more. This time we took photographs of the kit and labelled up each key component. One of my colleagues pointed out that our overseas colleague had in fact left us with some diagrams of the machine, but only an Engineer who was familiar with the equipment would be able to understand the diagrams. The visuals in an SOP have to be meaningful and be able to be understood at all levels in the business. This was the switch for us in the business from text only SOPs to visual based SOPs.

When it comes to your business you need to determine what kind of visual inclusions would work best for the people who will use the documents. The simplest way to do this is to offer them a range of options. Sometimes a photo is best; other times a diagram or sketch. A screen shot works well when you are referring to computer programs and sometimes part of a scanned document is a better option. Having these in the back of your mind when working with others to create SOPs is important as it enables you to suggest the most appropriate options when developing the instructions.

At the end of this book is a link to some downloads, presented in two formats that I have used successfully with my clients over the years. One is a PowerPoint format, which I have found to be better to use when there are multiple photos for a process. The other format is Word, which appears to be favoured when there are screenshots to be included in the document and / or more text required for the explanation. I recommend that you download both formats, play with them, and see what fits your needs best. And if you already have a format then have a look to see if there are any items you would like to include in your own documents.

One of the greatest benefits of moving to accurate visual SOPs is the ability to speed up the training progress of new staff, something we'll come back to in a few section's time.

COMPANY	Operating Instruction	Ref: SOP123
By: Giles Johnston	**Date:** 10 June 2012	**Issue:** 1
	Progress Review	

Synopsis:

This is the main program that allows purchase order review dates to be reviewed.

This instruction is used to progress review purchase orders.

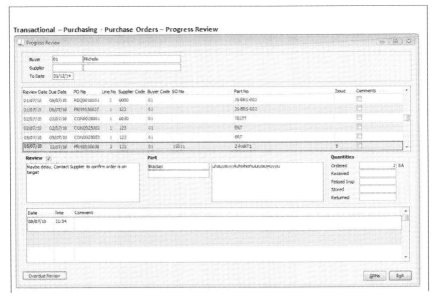

Example of a 'more' visual SOP

Who Should Write SOPs?

When writing SOPs it is generally agreed that it is best to get the person who does the task to write the SOP. I like this approach, but recognise that the person who is best at the job is not necessarily the person who can organise the information into a usable document. I like the approach of 'writing pairs' for SOPs.

Writing pairs is simply the notion that you get two perspectives on an SOP at the time of writing, from the person describing the way to do a job and the person who is recording the information. A simple example of this is to pair up a manufacturing operator with a process engineer. The operator knows all of the little oddities of the process; the engineer is usually more used to the writing of documents. That said it is likely that the engineer will also be familiar with the design elements of the process and be able to have a view on the information they are recording. This kind of partnership works well in most cases and can help both parties identify improvement opportunities for a process by getting a meeting of minds. That's right, writing SOPs can also be used to stimulate innovation within processes just from the effect of having a time out and reviewing what is being done currently (both the bad and the good).

Another good partnership is when a member of staff works with their manager to write an SOP. It is important to make the writing pairs equals for the duration of the SOP writing process in order for the open conversation to work best, and I realise that this is not always an easy thing to manage. From my experience, having two people work on the same SOP at the same time is a great opportunity to understand the issues being faced by your staff with a particular process, and as mentioned above, a great way to generate improvement ideas to make the process even more slick and efficient in the future.

Once an SOP has been written, having some form of sanity check is a good idea. Just because you and a colleague have written something it doesn't mean that it can be understood. A great test is to get someone who is unfamiliar with the process to follow your SOP. If they can do it without support then you know that you have written a high quality instruction. However, if you do find yourself being questioned constantly then use the opportunity to fine tune and clarify the points in your document until there are no more questions left. If there have been a number of points raised then you may want to re-run the exercise with another unsuspecting colleague to make sure the changes you have made are effective.

This kind of sanity checking doesn't need to be done all the time. As you get more proficient at writing these kinds of documents you will find that the need to test lessens. If I write SOPs with my clients then I still get them to test the information with their colleagues, as a 'best practice' if you like. In the next section we are going to look at some guidelines to make writing your SOPs simpler and more effective from the start.

SOP Writing Guidelines

Whilst writing SOPs isn't one of the greatest works of art in existence there is an art to writing these documents. This section covers a number of points to help you in writing more easily usable and effective tools for your business.

Setting the context is important. SOPs that aren't clear as to where they fit into the overall scheme of things are difficult to follow and this is a trap that experienced users of a system, or operators of a process, can fall in to. Just because you understand the background to a particular activity doesn't mean that the new person learning the role does, they may need to know why the document exists in order to choose to use it. We need to consider who is going to be using the document going forwards, and not just treating this as a 'box ticking' exercise. If you can start off the document with just a sentence or two to set the scene of the SOP it can make it much more accessible to those who are new to the activity.

Start at the start. Missing out a few basic steps at the start of the document is understandable if you are working on autopilot when you do your task, but for those of us who are learning how to complete a task, the first couple of steps make all the difference.

Similarly, detail each step in the process. Don't miss out any and, if you use specific shortcuts, make sure that they are accessible to the entire array of operators / users who will follow this instruction. As I'm sure you can imagine if you don't include a number of small steps then you can't complete the task without guessing how to fill the gaps.

Don't assume the reader's prior knowledge before they use an SOP. We sometimes make assumptions that our colleagues in the business know what we know and quite often this is not the case. Treat each SOP as though you were going to teach a ten year old child and you will probably be writing in a way that ensures that anyone can pick up the instructions quickly. This is not to be interpreted as condescending, aiming the SOP at this level means that anyone can pick up the instruction and is more of a 'best practice' than a derisory comment. If a random person can pick up and complete a task based on the SOP then it has met the standard.

Use plain language whenever possible. Making assumptions about the reading skills of the people who use SOPs isn't a good idea and it makes following them more difficult than necessary.

I once had to re-write a three month old SOP that I found in a factory I worked at because no one knew what 'contiguous' meant. I changed it to 'overlap' and the SOP was accepted by the team. Thankfully the potential quality problem was avoided through the operators guessing what they had to do, but otherwise it could have been a significant issue for the business. I'm just glad that someone finally spoke up and complained about the wording. So, if you are faced with a long or usual word please try to find a replacement.

Leave the theory (or philosophy) out of the document. The SOP should be a finite series of steps to get you from the start of the process to the end of the process. Occasionally I find SOPs that are written about the general subject and it tells you about all of the options you have available to you. The purpose of the SOP is to share the optimum process. It isn't there to share a whole raft of theories or open ended options about what you could do to complete the process. Although this issue is less common than the other issues in this section it is still worth looking out for if you have people who are unsure of the process that they are managing / executing that are then tasked to write the SOP.

Use visuals to reduce the amount of writing required. As

discussed in an earlier section, the use of photos, scans, diagrams etc. can make understanding a SOP far easier than if they weren't present. I know that sometimes it can be quite hard to think of what images to include if there is not something obvious or physical to photograph, that's when a good sketch can come in useful. A couple of good images can dramatically drop the amount of words you require to write a good SOP and I'd encourage you to start incorporating them if you don't already.

Even though we may write excellent SOPs there is still a fair chance that people either don't follow what you have written, can't read what you've written, or just can't be bothered. Although we'll deal with SOPs as a training tool in a moment we can give people the opportunity to put their hands up to ask for help. A common, and effective, way of doing this is to emphasise the phrase 'IF IN DOUBT – ASK!!' somewhere on the document and link it back to the training when the SOPs are issued / revised. Even with the best SOP writer in the world I still believe that someone somewhere will still find an issue that needs to be resolved and we need to make sure that we get people putting their hands up and asking for help at the appropriate time.

Acronyms are a way of life in many businesses and therefore we need to explain acronyms when we introduce them for the initiated. The minimum we need to do is to use the full length phrase at the start of the document and put the initials, or acronym, in brackets afterwards. You may choose to add a glossary at the end of the SOP instead, or hold that information centrally. Whatever you choose to do please try to be consistent and make it easily accessible for new readers of your SOPs.

To help with the revision control and updating of the SOPs it is incredibly useful to have the date of writing and the author(s) listed at the start of the document. This is fairly common practice, but I still manage to find the occasional business that has instructions where the operators don't know how old the information is, or who to turn to when they have a question about the process. Please make sure that you aren't one of the few businesses who commit this sin!

Although this section may seem obvious to you I felt I couldn't leave it out as I see too many bad examples on my travels. So, let's leave this section now and move on to more ways to make SOPs work for your business.

Creating the 'SOP' Map

One of the issues that I have seen businesses struggle with is making sense out of all of the SOPs that they written over the years. Often the indexes / registers are full of documents that were written at different times and so don't have a logical flow to the sequences. Businesses that have started their SOPs from scratch have the opportunity to provide a numbering / reference system that allows them to simply group documents together. Of course you still may have the issue that the numbers within the sub-groups get out of sequence, but it is a better approach overall. By creating a simple 'SOP' map you can provide a very simple method of locating the correct SOP for the task in hand should the information not be present in a work instruction / production routing or similar.

An example of a simple 'SOP' map for a process

Putting SOPs into context can be useful as a reference point. A simple graphical flow of the SOPs and how they fit together in sequence is great for training purposes and allows for better understanding of the process.

The issue I am addressing here is similar to that of a hard disk fragmenting with use. The various files on the computer get moved around so that the files required by one program get split up and moved apart. Defragmenting the hard disk allows the related files to be located next to each other once more, speeding up the computer. Whilst we probably don't want to arrange our files in their correct sequence, a simple guide to the flow of SOPs can make life a lot easier.

Extending the idea of an 'SOP' map is that of using the format to create appropriate hyperlinks to increase the accessibility of the SOP documents. Even a simple list of the SOPs in a Word document can be transformed into a linked document allowing fast access into the bowels of your computer network. Fast access can often mean increased usage. Many businesses have their SOPs located so far down a directory structure that only the IT people know where they are.

It's the idea that is important, more than the format. But to get you started I have included a downloadable template for your consideration. Please find it in the 'Downloads' section near the end of this book.

Organising the SOPs through meaning makes the instructions visible once again to the people that they affect. If we think about the problem for long enough we can make it simpler and more practical for the people that need to know this information. I hope that if you use this approach you come up with a clean, simple design that works for you.

Using SOPs as a Training Aid

SOPs can be the backbone of a good training programme.

I have seen new people join a team within a business, be handed a compiled pack of SOPs that have been well thought out and written and get started being productive in their office role within hours.

I have seen new people join a team within a business, be given someone to shadow for a while and still not be competent one year later.

SOPs can be a sign off tool for training programmes for new starters or for people who are mature in their role. By including a simple sign off sheet that details the SOPs that currently affect their role which they can sign to say that they understand the instructions and will comply with them, you can have a simple approach that helps to ensure that people who need to ask questions ask them.

It also helps to have discussions when people have drifted off course and need to be reminded of the correct process.

I'm not advocating this as a route to let you beat up your staff, but by building a sign off process like this into your training provisions you can have a more objective conversation later on.

A manufacturing team in a business that I worked at had a raft of new people joining them due to an expansion of the firm. The process was technical in nature and the SOPs had all been revised to include more accurate information and photos of the various pieces of equipment. I created a cover sheet for the department's copy of the SOPs which had a space for each operator in the team to sign off against. Training for the new operators was faster than we had experienced previously and there were no objections to the inclusion of the sign off element. We did have a few incidents where we needed to remind people of the SOP and, because they had signed off on the cover sheet the conversation was very easy and straightforward to have.

Build SOPs into Your Routines

Once you have SOPs written that meet the needs of your business and you have added them into your training / staff inductions you then have the opportunity to further improve the visibility of the SOPs by building them into your workplace routines.

The weekly routine is a common tool where a flexible 'timetable' is created. If you have read my other books you will know that I like routines. Of course I am not talking about a rigid timetable that removes all of the creativity and 'wiggle room' in a person's diary, but a gentle reminder that certain things need to happen at specific points in time. The timetable is largely developed from the understanding and clarification of what the business processes you operate need to do at each stage of the process and by whom. Defining the key inputs and outputs of each stage can help you to create this simple routine and in doing so you create an alternative SOP map that is reflected against each role rather than by process flow.

Linking each routine to its SOP is a simple case of listing all of the tasks that need to happen as part of a specific person's routine and including the SOP reference after each task. Then provide everyone with a copy of the routine so that they can develop the right kinds of habits and have an easy reference to the associated SOP.

This is a simple approach that can make a big difference.

	MRP CONTROLLER
Daily	Release works orders / Oversee printing of job cards (SOP No 53) Ensure previous day S/O Book is printed off and place overdues on re-plan date (SOP No 54) Update planned ship dates and comments from feedback received on Works order changes form (SOP No 55) Update on hold and re-plan date and Circulate (SOP No 55) Prioritisation of parts *as required* (SOP No 52) Manually Run MRP and Scheduling (SOP No 51)
Monday	Production Control Meeting
Tuesday	
Wednesday	On Hold Meeting
Thursday	Housekeeping (SOP No 58)
Friday	Produce / print off all KPI'S -Capacity Plan -MPS -System KPI's
Weekly / Monthly / Quarterly	

Example of a timetable including SOP references

Reviewing and Updating Your SOPs

As discussed at start of this book, out of date SOPs are an absolute killer to having a system that actually benefits your business. Periodically these documents need to be reviewed, they need to be updated to include the most relevant and optimal methods of working. In many cases I find that the SOPs don't get updated in line with their shelf life and are instead updated when someone finds a problem with a process and tracks it back to the SOP's information. If you have been successful however, and the SOPs are now becoming part of the normal working life within your business, then you have a good chance that these documents are being used and referred to more often, potentially heading off the problem of the documents not being up to date.

Updating SOPs is something that can be simple to do, and I'll share with you my thoughts on how to do this.

Firstly, build the review into your routines. We discussed in the previous section about linking the SOPs to the routines / timetable that you can use with your department to keep everything ticking over. Adding in the review of SOPs is no different. Possibly once a month or once a quarter this task could be actioned. Let me explain further.

Most businesses have some kind of SOP register, detailing the current revision / issue level, the author and the date of writing. This is often held within a spreadsheet or database and lends itself to adding in three more columns of information.

The first column would be for a reviewed date. This would be the date that the SOP was reviewed for relevance and accuracy as opposed to the date that it was created.

The second additional column could be used to give each SOP a shelf life. Depending on the maturity of the SOP could affect how long you want to leave it before you review the document. If the SOP is new then perhaps you want to review it in 30 days and slowly relax it out as you become comfortable to 90 days, to 180 days, to 365 days. A yearly revision of SOPs can work well as long as the revisions are staggered appropriately. To make life easier for both of us, I am going to assume that you are using a spreadsheet. Use days as the interval and enter the appropriate number of days (as described a moment ago) in the column.

The third additional column could then be a simple formula to determine if today's date is greater than the revision date plus the shelf life 'interval'. If it is greater, the formula could flag up a 'review me!' message or similar. For you spreadsheet boffins out there it would look something like:

=if(now()>('review date' + 'shelf life'),"review me!","")

I have included a quick example spreadsheet in the downloads should you want to explore this option further. Feel free to play with the dates and shelf life to see how it works. Depending on when you buy this book will depend on how the formulas respond. Please feel free to change the review dates accordingly!

So, to make this work as part of the routine, the responsible person would review the SOP register to see which SOPs require review and then that list can be brought to the relevant team meeting and the work shared out accordingly. It's not difficult stuff to do, but once again this is about making SOPs part of the normal day to day working and keeping them in the spotlight to maintain good working standards.

Stability of Processes

As we get near the end of this guide to making SOPs more useful and more visible within the business I think it is worth mentioning the stability of processes over time.

It is quite common for processes to 'drift' as time passes. You know the situation, you start asking someone about the key steps in a process and then you find that the process isn't followed. What you do find out is that someone thought that a different process would work better and they adopted that. Trying to manage the enthusiasm of someone wanting to change a process alongside having a system that is under control is one of the tasks that any leader must deal with.

Of course, if a process isn't working then we should look into correcting this situation as quickly as possible. We don't want to wait until we get a really unpleasant phone call from a customer (or worse) before we change a process. However I am talking about the smaller iterations of a process, things that won't cause any major changes but ones that potentially improve a process' performance.

If we go back to the idea of routines then we can consider the iteration of SOPs as a revolving process where we stock up the ideas and innovations for a process and discuss them at a regular improvement meeting. There are two really good reasons for waiting to improve a SOP in a formal meeting environment.

Firstly, if the SOP is new then, unless something is drastically wrong with the instruction, it is sometimes helpful to stick with the process until you have some more information. Changing the instructions and / or the way you do things because people aren't familiar with a process, or haven't practised it enough times yet is not a good reason to change the SOP. I have seen this happen numerous times, so it is worth ensuring that the change is due to valid reasons and not just because of a lack of experience with the SOP. Getting the whole team involved with the validation of a SOP is a good way to quickly get this feedback.

Secondly, if the changes to the SOP are made without involving other people in the decision making process, you could be introducing problems to people down the line in the overall business process. Describing the changes at a formal session where others in the process are present can be used as a 'go / no go' check to ensure that the revision is acceptable. I have also seen this time and time again; where a well meaning member of staff has figured out a way to improve a process step and then has gone on to implement the change without informing anyone else in the process. You've guessed it, the next person down the line then can't do their job properly, or can do it but with more difficulty. Getting the balance right is the aim of the game.

Agreeing upon a period of stability that the team can work with is key. Keep the ideas until the next time the improvement meeting (or whatever vehicle you choose to use) comes around and then introduce the changes as they are seen fit. This period of stability that I refer to is the same as the 'shelf life' that I mentioned in the previous section. New SOPs can have a short shelf life so that you can ensure that the right process is embedded and more mature SOPs can have longer shelf lives.

Agree changes as a team and write them up as a team as discussed earlier too.

I suppose I should end this section by saying don't stop the experimenting. Finding better ways of working needs to be encouraged and that's what you get to do in-between the revision process. It's not the ideas and motivation that are bad, problems arise when the control is lost over the processes and either the SOPs aren't agreed or the process doesn't resemble the SOPs.

Closing Remarks

I hope from reading this book you have gained some new ideas or insights about how you can make SOPs work more effectively for your business.

SOPs can be an amazing tool to speed up learning, maintain quality of processes and embed the innovations generated during your business' ongoing continuous improvement activities.

SOPs are not designed to slow down a business, or make it more bureaucratic, they are there to support your business in becoming more effective, increasing the profits and making life a little easier overall.

To summarise what we have covered in this book, we have looked at:

• How SOPs can benefit your business, from managing quality aspects to sealing off improvement projects.

• Why SOPs are often inadequate and why they aren't used in the way that they should be.

• The benefits of including better graphics into a SOP, to improve the document's clarity and effectiveness.

• Using writing pairs to enable more effective SOPs to be written, potentially marrying the best knowledge with the best writer.

• Guidelines to make sure that your SOPs can be understood once written.

• Creating a 'SOP map' to help provide a better understanding of the SOPs and how they fit together.

• Linking SOPs to training and staff inductions so that we can shorten the time it takes to become effective within a role.

• Building SOPs into the routine within your business / department so that you can make these documents part of normal working life rather than a one off exercise.

• Developing an index, or register, of SOPs that can help you to manage the revision and 'process management' process more easily.

• Keeping the reins on the processes when you have lots and lots of potential improvements you can make to your SOPs.

We've covered a lot of ground in a short time and I hope you have found it to be useful.

Please play with the ideas and come up with your own combinations and experiments until you find the methods that work for you and your business.

Downloads

These downloads require you to have some experience with the programs in the first place. The downloads should be fairly self explanatory, some specific additional points are detailed below the link.

The files include:

- SOP format – Microsoft Powerpoint
- SOP format – Microsoft Word
- Sign off sheet – Microsoft Word
- SOP map – Microsoft PowerPoint
- SOP register – Microsoft Excel

Please visit: **http://www.smartspeed.co.uk/sops/sops.php**

How to adjust the details of the slide 'structure' in the PowerPoint SOP format*

Click on the 'Slide Master' option as a presentation view.

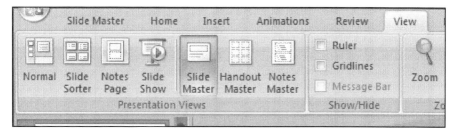

Ensure that you select the highest level in the Slide Master 'tree' before you edit the contents.

Change the necessary details by clicking on the corresponding text boxes and update with your details.

Close the Slide Master, using the 'Close Master View' from the 'Slide Master' tab.

How to add a new slide in the PowerPoint SOP format*

Right click on a slide that you want to duplicate. Choose 'Duplicate Slide' from the pop out menu.

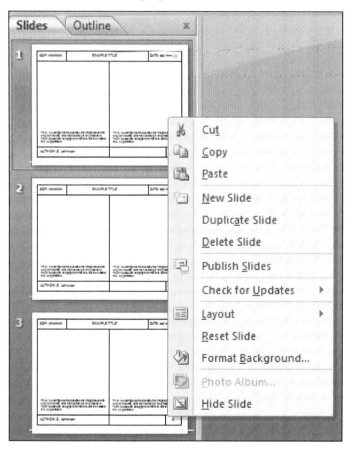

* Screenshots taken from the 2007 version of Microsoft Office.

Links and Resources

Smartspeed Blog

For more ideas on how to improve your business and to find out how to apply some of the more common business improvement ideas in novel ways please visit our blog:

http://www.smartspeed.info

Free On Time Delivery Report

If you want some ideas around improving the on time delivery performance of your business, then please download our free report. You will need to register your email address on our website, the link is:

http://www.systemsandprocesses.co.uk

LinkedIn OTIF Forum

If you would like to join us online to discuss practical ideas around improving on time delivery performance then please visit our LinkedIn group:

http://www.linkedin.com/groups/On-Time-Delivery-Improvement-4419220/about

'Making It Happen' online course

Discover practical change management strategies with this 30 module online course, aimed at accelerating the rate of change at your place of work.

http://www.making-it-happen.website

About Giles Johnston

Giles is a Chartered Engineer with a background in Operations Management. He spends most of his time working on capacity planning and 'on time delivery' improvement projects.

Giles has worked in a variety of different roles within manufacturing and as a consultant for a prestigious university.

In 2005 Giles decided to forge his own path and created Smartspeed, which has been helping businesses to improve their delivery performance, along with their profits, ever since.

Giles can be contacted by:

Email -   **gilesjohnston@smartspeed.co.uk**

Website -   **www.smartspeed.co.uk**

Made in the USA
Middletown, DE
14 April 2023

28874010R00038